THIS BOOK BELONGS TO

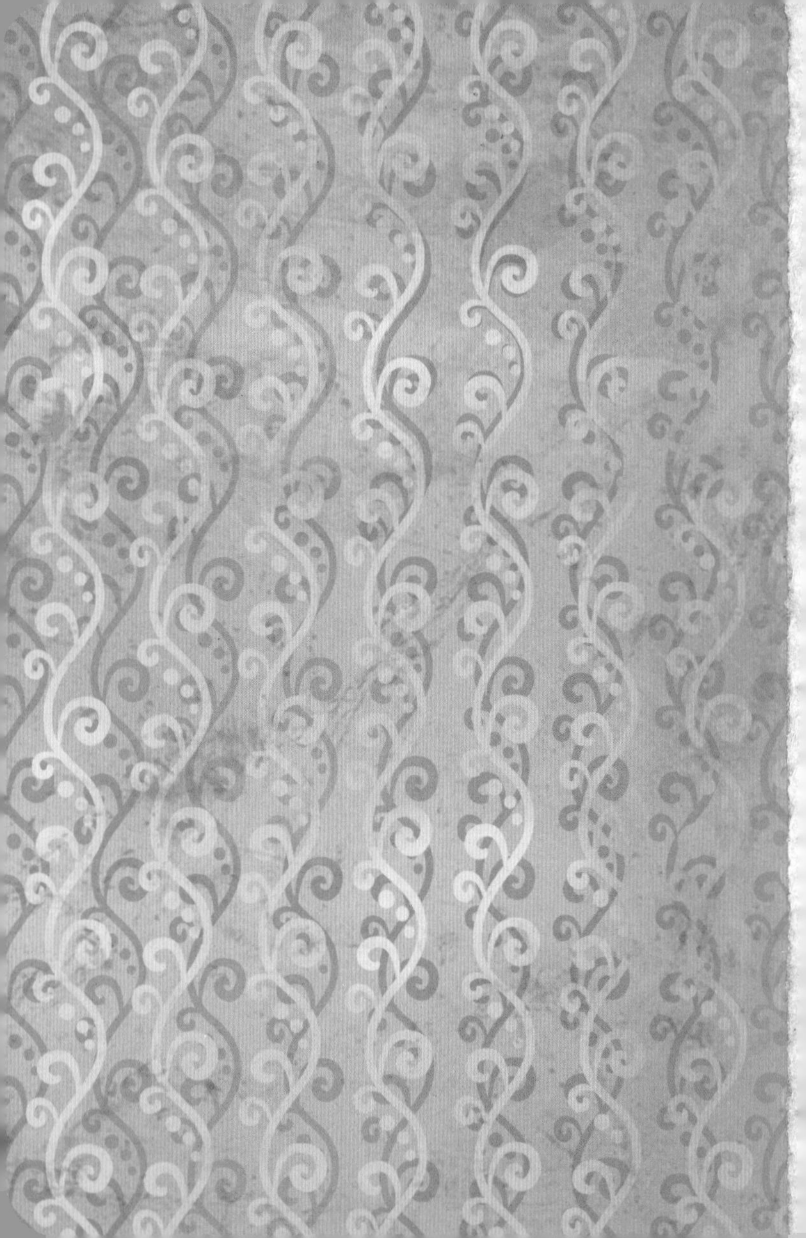

PRAYERS & PROMISES

for Grandmas

BroadStreet
PUBLISHING

CONTENTS

Introduction

Prayers & Promises for Grandmas incorporates more than 70 themes that help you connect with your Creator in many different areas of your life.

This beautifully designed book gives you easy access to God's promises about faithfulness, trust, wisdom, worth, beauty, strength, and much more, with uplifting prayers and thought-provoking questions for deeper reflection.

By staying connected to God, and believing the promises of his Word, you can live a fulfilling, blessed life in close relationship with your heavenly Father and be an amazing encouragement to your grandchildren as well.

Acceptance

"The Father gives me the people who are mine.
Every one of them will come to me,
and I will always accept them."

John 6:37 NCV

The Lord does not see as man sees; for man looks at the outward appearance, but the Lord looks at the heart.

1 Samuel 16:7 NKJV

If God is for us, who can be against us?

Romans 8:31 ESV

Before he made the world, God chose us to be his very own through what Christ would do for us; he decided then to make us holy in his eyes, without a single fault—we who stand before him covered with his love.

Ephesians 1:4 TLB

It is wonderful, Lord, that you accept me just as I am. I don't have to try to be something more or prove to anyone that I am adequate. You created me in your image—mind, body and spirit—to live in a loving relationship with you. You are not impressed by my successes or disappointed in my shortcomings. Covered with your love, I am gently conformed to your image. Help me to show this same love and acceptance to my grandchildren.

I pray too, Lord, that my grandkids would embrace this truth—that they would understand that they are unique creations of a loving God who made them just right. Help them not to compare themselves to others or try to be like someone else. Let them be content in who they are.

How does God's acceptance of you help you to be more accepting of others?

Anger

Don't get angry.
Don't be upset; it only leads to trouble.
Evil people will be sent away,
but those who trust the LORD will inherit the land.

PSALM 37:8-9 NCV

Everyone should be quick to listen,
slow to speak and slow to become angry,
because human anger does not produce
the righteousness that God desires.

JAMES 1:19-20 NIV

"Don't sin by letting anger control you."
Don't let the sun go down while you are still angry.

EPHESIANS 4:26 NLT

Lord Jesus, forgive me for the times I have given my tongue too much liberty and said things that were unkind, unloving, or hurtful. Sometimes to justify myself, I call my anger "frustration" as if the change in semantics makes it any less sinful. So often I jump to conclusions, make judgments, and fail to listen to the whole story. Help me to listen more, slow down my response, corral my tongue, and allow your Holy Spirit to be in charge.

God, at times I see my grandkids get carried away by their anger and behave in ways that are selfish and spiteful. Give their parents patience and wisdom to deal with the outbursts in a mature and godly way. Help them to learn self-control so as they grow, they will not be controlled by anger.

What does it mean to be quick to listen and slow to speak?

Anxiety

You will keep in perfect peace those whose minds are steadfast, because they trust in you.

Isaiah 26:3 NIV

"Don't let your hearts be troubled. Trust in God, and trust also in me."

John 14:1 NLT

Give all your worries to him, because he cares about you.

1 Peter 5:7 NCV

I call out to the Lord when I'm in trouble, and he answers me.

Psalm 120:1 NIRV

Lord, thank you for peace that passes understanding. It is mine for the taking if I keep my mind focused on you, trust you more, and cast all my worries on you. In difficult moments, it is easy for me to forget how faithful you have been to me in the past. Instead of dwelling on those victories, I tend to ruminate on the unknowns and the what-ifs. So today once again, I throw all of my cares on your shoulders and resolve to let your peace reign in my heart!

My grandchildren have a different set of worries and fears than mine. Theirs revolve around the darkness at night, going to the doctor, mom and dad going away, or the first day of school. I ask that today you would surround them with your peace that settles deep down in their hearts. Remove all fear and give them rest.

What steps can you take to be less anxious and more trusting?

Beauty

You are altogether beautiful, my darling,
beautiful in every way.

Song of Songs 4:7 NLT

No, your beauty should come from within you—
the beauty of a gentle and quiet spirit that will never
be destroyed and is very precious to God.

1 Peter 3:4 NCV

She puts on strength and honor
as if they were her clothes.
She can laugh at the days that are coming.

Proverbs 31:25 NIRV

I praise you because you made me
in an amazing and wonderful way.
What you have done is wonderful. I know this very well.

Psalm 139:14 NCV

Throughout my life, God, I have spent much time and money on my outward appearance. You put the desire for beauty in my nature, so looking good is not in itself sinful. But the truth is, beauty comes from within and is reflected outwardly. Help me to develop the beauty of a deeper relationship with you so that your love and kindness would be mirrored on my face. As the years tick by, and age takes its toll, may your beauty be increasingly seen in me.

Jesus, you have created my wonderful grandchildren—thank you for them. As they grow and mature through the years, I pray that they would see themselves as you see them—beautiful. Help them be content with who you made them to be. Help them not to compare themselves to others or despise their reflection, but instead, work on developing true inner beauty through your Word and prayer.

How does it make you feel to think God sees you as beautiful?

Blessings

Surely, LORD, you bless those who do what is right.
Like a shield, your loving care keeps them safe.

PSALM 5:12 NIRV

Surely you have granted him unending blessings
and made him glad with the joy of your presence.

PSALM 21:6 NIV

Give praise to the God and Father of our Lord Jesus Christ. He has blessed us with every spiritual blessing. Those blessings come from the heavenly world. They belong to us because we belong to Christ. God chose us to belong to Christ before the world was created. He chose us to be holy and without blame in his eyes. He loved us.

EPHESIANS 1:3–4 NIRV

I am so grateful today, God, for the blessings you continue to pour into my life. Your goodness comes to me in a myriad of ways—through my children and grandchildren, through friends and relatives, but ultimately all from your hand. I am undeserving, especially when I remember the many times I've been ungrateful and wallowed in self-pity. Instead of a frown from you, I get a hug from my grandbaby, a slobbery kiss from my preschooler, a helping hand from one of your followers. You continue to amaze me with unexpected joys. Thank you, Jesus.

Teach my grandchildren to be grateful. They have so much more than I ever had as a child, but sometimes the more they have, the more they want. Help their parents to be wise in their giving and careful to teach their kids gratitude.

Which of God's blessings come to your mind today?

Boldness

He proclaimed the kingdom of God
and taught about the Lord Jesus Christ—
with all boldness and without hindrance!

Acts 28:31 NIV

Sinners run away even when no one is chasing them.
But those who do what is right are as bold as lions.

Proverbs 28:1 NIrV

On the day I called you, you answered me.
You made me strong and brave.

Psalm 138:3 NCV

So let us come boldly to the throne of our gracious God.
There we will receive his mercy,
and we will find grace to help us when we need it most.

Hebrews 4:16 NLT

How I love your invitation to run to your throne boldly to find the help I need! There is just no God like you. Thank you for giving me strength and courage when I cry out to you. I need boldness to share the Gospel with others; I need strength physically and emotionally when I'm facing a hard time; I need to be brave when you ask me to do something outside of my comfort zone. Standing strong in the middle of a godless culture isn't easy.

And for my precious grandkids, help them to be strong and brave and willing to stand alone if they must in a world that has no regard for you. They are facing unprecedented pressure to conform. They rub shoulders with peers and teachers who do not know you and are vocal in their unbelief. Make them bold as lions but gentle as lambs.

Why is it sometimes hard to be bold?

Caring

If anyone has material possessions and sees a brother or sister in need but has no pity on them, how can the love of God be in that person? Dear children, let us not love with words or speech but with actions and in truth.

1 John 3:17-18 NIV

"I was hungry. And you gave me something to eat. I was thirsty. And you gave me something to drink. I was a stranger. And you invited me in. I needed clothes. And you gave them to me. I was sick. And you took care of me. I was in prison. And you came to visit me. …The King will reply, 'What I'm about to tell you is true. Anything you did for one of the least important of these brothers and sisters of mine, you did for me.'"

Matthew 25:35-36, 40 NIRV

God, give me a heart for others like you have. In your time on earth you had compassion on the blind, the lame, and the sick. You loved little kids; you had empathy for the poor, and mercy on the sinner. I want a heart like that. I'm too quick to judge or too busy to lend a hand or visit the sick. My own agenda too often comes first and I forget that when I do something for the needy, I'm actually doing it for you.

Jesus, give my grandkids a heart for others. May they be the unusual ones who let others go first, who stop and help a little one tie a shoe, and who let friends have their way. Help them not to be so self-absorbed and petty, but learn to put others first. Do your work in their hearts as only you can do.

How can you care for someone else today?

Change

Look! I tell you this secret:
We will not all sleep in death,
but we will all be changed.

1 Corinthians 15:51 NCV

He will take our weak mortal bodies and change them into glorious bodies like his own, using the same power with which he will bring everything under his control.

Philippians 3:21 NLT

Jesus Christ is the same
yesterday and today and forever.

Hebrews 13:8 NIrV

Lord, I am really looking forward to that new body you promise us. Every year that goes by and with each new ache and pain, I am reminded that this earthly body is indeed temporary, and I need a new glorious body that will last forever. In the meantime, help me to eat right, sleep enough, and exercise so that I can stay healthy until the day my work on this earth is completed. Help me to chat with you about my ailments rather than those around me.

My grandkids wear me out at times by their youthful vigor. I am so grateful you made them healthy and strong. When childhood illnesses bring them down, or more serious issues come, help them to trust you through it. May they understand that their bodies are yours. Protect them from substance abuse and sexual impurity that would defile them. Thank you, Jesus.

Is there anything more you can do to stay strong and healthy?

Children

Direct your children onto the right path,
and when they are older, they will not leave it.

Proverbs 22:6 NLT

These words which I command you today shall be in your heart. You shall teach them diligently to your children, and shall talk of them when you sit in your house, when you walk by the way, when you lie down, and when you rise up.

Deuteronomy 6:6–7 NKJV

"Let the little children come to Me, and do not forbid them; for of such is the kingdom of heaven."

Matthew 19:14 NKJV

Children are a gift from the Lord;
they are a reward from him.

Psalm 127:3 NLT

God, I want to be a part of directing my grandkids onto the right path so when they are older, they will not leave it! Would you reawaken memories of your faithfulness to me through the years so I can share them? My stories of your intervention, provision, and healing power can then become a part of their faith foundation to be built upon as they experience your work in their lives.

Give my grandkids a heart for you. May they always walk in your ways, run to you in times of trouble, and trust you with every fiber of their being.

Can you encourage your grandchildren in the Lord today?

Compassion

When I am with those who are weak, I share their weakness, for I want to bring the weak to Christ. Yes, I try to find common ground with everyone, doing everything I can to save some.

1 Corinthians 9:22 NLT

God, have mercy on me according to your faithful love.
Because your love is so tender and kind,
wipe out my lawless acts.

Psalm 51:1 NIRV

Praise be to the God and Father of our Lord Jesus Christ, the Father of compassion and the God of all comfort.

2 Corinthians 1:3 NIV

Thank you, God, for the many times you have comforted me in my sorrow, strengthened me in my weakness, and loved me in spite of my failings. I want to be like that. I want my heart to hurt when I see others hurting; I want to show compassion to the weak and the unlovely. Soften my heart; remove all indifference so your love can flow freely to others.

God, I melt when I see one of my grandchildren share a toy, look out for a sibling, or be a peacemaker. I know you smile when one of your precious little ones shows the love and care of Jesus. Continue to open their hearts to the needs of others. Teach them to put aside their selfishness and become the people you want them to be.

How can you be a more compassionate person?

Confidence

I can do everything through Christ,
who gives me strength.

PHILIPPIANS 4:13 NLT

Be my rock of refuge,
to which I can always go;
give the command to save me,
for you are my rock and my fortress….
For You have been my hope, Sovereign LORD,
my confidence since my youth.

PSALM 71:3, 5 NIV

Do not throw away your confidence,
which has a great reward.

HEBREWS 10:35 NCV

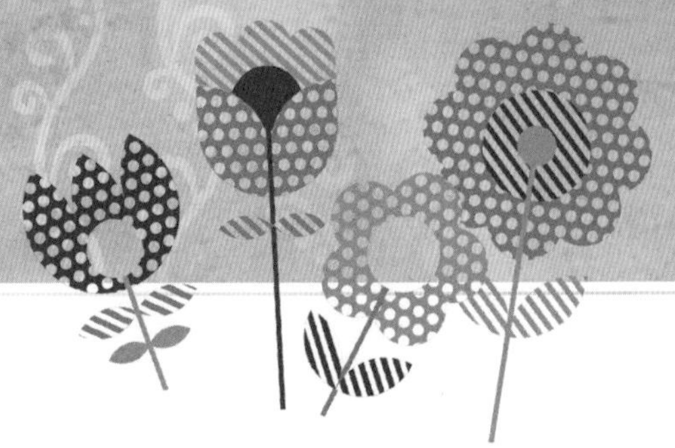

Thank you, God, for never asking me to do anything you do not give me strength and confidence to do. I've wondered at times whether or not you really know what you are doing. In the natural, I am weak and afraid. At times I have thought I would come unglued with fear! But together we make it through. We've been through a lot of scary situations. I love you, Lord. You have always been my rock, my hope, and my confidence.

I pray now for my grandchildren. Deliver them from all irrational fears. May their trust in you grow bigger than their anxieties, and may they run to you with all their troubles. Help them to know that you are their place of safety.

How do you find your confidence?

Contentment

To enjoy your work and to accept your lot in life—
that is indeed a gift from God.
The person who does that will not need to look back
with sorrow on his past, for God gives him joy.

Ecclesiastes 5:20 TLB

I know what it is to be in need, and I know what it is to have plenty. I have learned the secret of being content in any and every situation, whether well fed or hungry, whether living in plenty or in want. I can do all this through him who gives me strength.

Philippians 4:12-13 NIV

God, contentment with my life and circumstances is getting easier as the years go by. I have seen your faithfulness in every situation. I thank you for providing numerous opportunities to learn this lesson through unemployment, financial difficulties, sickness, and loss. I choose to be satisfied with each moment you have orchestrated. Forgive me when I compare myself to others and miss the joy of the moment.

My grandkids, Lord, live a world of affluence and are surrounded by those who have the best and newest gadgets. Can you bring them safely through this season where it may seem that others have it better? Help them choose contentment for the blessings they already have and deliver them from the sorrow discontent brings.

How can you choose to be content with your life as it is right now?

Courage

Be strong in the Lord and in his mighty power.
Put on the full armor of God, so that you can take your stand against the devil's schemes.

EPHESIANS 6:10-11 NIV

Be alert. Continue strong in the faith.
Have courage, and be strong. Do everything in love.

1 CORINTHIANS 16:13-14 NCV

Even though I walk through the darkest valley,
I will not be afraid. You are with me.
Your shepherd's rod and staff comfort me.

PSALM 23:4 NIRV

"This is my command—be strong and courageous!
Do not be afraid or discouraged.
For the LORD your God is with you wherever you go."

JOSHUA 1:9 NLT

Courage does not come naturally to me, God. You know that by nature I am fearful, reticent to try new things, and at times have wished you had made me differently. I envy those who relish change and seem to charge into the unknown with enthusiasm. As I recall though, you have provided what was needed for every battle and every dark valley I have experienced in my lifetime. You have made me strong and courageous just at the right times.

Jesus, I pray for my grandchildren as they face battles I never had to face. Satan's tactics are more insidious than ever. Make the kids strong in your power and give them courage to stand alone when necessary. Help them make the hard choices and refuse to compromise. May they grow up to be mighty men and women of God.

When was the last time you asked God for courage?

Courtesy

Each of us should please our neighbors for their good, to build them up. For even Christ did not please himself but, as it is written: "The insults of those who insult you have fallen on me."

Romans 15:2–3 NIV

Welcome strangers, because some who have done this have welcomed angels without knowing it.

Hebrews 13:2 NCV

Remind God's people to obey rulers and authorities. Remind them to be ready to do what is good. Tell them not to speak evil things against anyone. Remind them to live in peace. They must consider the needs of others. They must always be gentle toward everyone.

Titus 3:1–2 NIRV

Lord Jesus, your Word challenges me today. I want to be more like you and treat others with kindness, courtesy and love—whether friend, neighbor, or stranger. Sometimes I feel awkward with those I don't know or those who are different. Other times my own judgments and opinions keep people at a distance. Help me to spend more time focusing on others and less on myself. I want to imitate you well.

Help my grandchildren to be good to their siblings, classmates, and friends. It's easy for them to join in when others are badgering or bullying a peer. Help them to reach out to the new kid in town with encouragement and friendship, not to retaliate, and to be gentle to all. Teach them to obey those in authority so others can follow their lead.

Why is it sometimes difficult to place the needs of your grandchildren before your own?

Creativity

Lord, you have made many things;
with your wisdom you made them all.
The earth is full of your riches.

Psalm 104:24 NCV

We are God's masterpiece.
He has created us anew in Christ Jesus,
so we can do the good things he planned for us long ago.

Ephesians 2:10 NLT

The Lord has filled him with the Spirit of God.
He has filled him with wisdom, with understanding,
with knowledge and with all kinds of skill.

Exodus 35:31 NIRV

We have different gifts,
according to the grace given to each of us.

Romans 12:6 NIV

Thank you, God, for the masterpiece that is me! I don't see myself that way, but I am so thankful that your love covers all the imperfections. What a joy to know that you have created me anew and even planned the good things you wanted me to do during my life on earth. Not only that, you filled me with your Spirit, with wisdom, understanding, knowledge, and all kinds of skills so I can accomplish those things. When I feel inadequate for a task, remind me of these truths.

My grandchildren are your masterpieces as well. How awesome it is to watch each of them develop in their own unique way. In one you put a love of music, in another unusual creativity, in another a love for books and learning. Each one is gifted by you. Help them to develop the talents you've given them and live them out for your glory.

How can you use your creativity for God?

Delight

When I received your words, I ate them.
They filled me with joy. My heart took delight in them.
LORD God who rules over all, I belong to you.

JEREMIAH 15:16 NIRV

"My God, I want to do what you want.
Your teachings are in my heart."

PSALM 40:8 NCV

Your laws are my treasure;
they are my heart's delight.

PSALM 119:111 NLT

"Let your light shine before others, that they may see your good deeds and glorify your Father in heaven."

MATTHEW 5:16 NIV

Your Word, God, is truly a treasure to me. Thank you for the indescribable riches found there and for how it speaks directly from your heart to mine. Sometimes though, I admit there is a gap between what I know and how I live. I want to live out your teachings, but frankly I'm often too busy to read, meditate, and pray, allowing your Word to do its work in my life. I want others to see your light through me and ultimately glorify your name.

Instill a love for your Word in my grandchildren, I pray. May they memorize it with delight so your instructions are written on their hearts. Bring your words to mind when they are faced with tough decisions. May they be happy to do your will.

Are you spending time in God's Word and letting it transform you?

Depression

The LORD hears his people when they call to him for help.
He rescues them from all their troubles.

PSALM 34:17 NLT

Why am I so sad?
Why am I so upset?
I should put my hope in God
and keep praising him.

PSALM 42:11 NCV

You, O LORD, are a shield about me,
my glory, and the lifter of my head.

PSALM 3:3 ESV

He has delivered us from the power of darkness and conveyed us into the kingdom of the Son of His love.

COLOSSIANS 1:13 NKJV

I am so grateful, God, that you rescue me from myself! The troubles of my soul are often of my own making as I dwell on the negative and agonize over the "if only." You are the God for all of me—body, mind, spirit, and emotion and only you can bring solutions to the many troubles unique to each part. You always rescue me when I call; you encourage me to persevere and to keep putting my hope in you. You are the one who holds my head high.

Help my grandkids to reach out to you when they are sad, lonely, or feeling insignificant or inadequate. When rivalry between classmates and peers occurs, please help them to look up. Keep them from drowning in darkness and sadness. Hold their heads high in the hard times.

Can you sense God's comfort and joy in the middle of your sadness today?

Devotion

"Whoever wants to be my disciple must deny themselves and take up their cross and follow me."

MATTHEW 16:24 NIV

"No servant can serve two masters.
The servant will hate one master and love the other,
or will follow one master and refuse to follow the other.
You cannot serve both God and worldly riches."

LUKE 16:13 NCV

Don't copy the behavior and customs of this world, but let God transform you into a new person by changing the way you think. Then you will learn to know God's will for you, which is good and pleasing and perfect.

ROMANS 12:2 NLT

Although some may say that the cost of following you is too high, God, I would rather be your disciple than serve the god of this world and pay the consequences. How can I put a price tag on forgiveness, eternal life, joy, or purpose? Help me to say no to myself and yes to your good and perfect will. When sacrifice is required, give me the grace to lay down my own desires and follow you devotedly.

Jesus, please do a deep work in my grandchildren as they grow. Saying no to themselves is just about the biggest challenge they will ever have. Give them the desire to be 100% yours, to follow you with their whole hearts. Make material things lose their luster. Help them to understand that your will for them is good, pleasing, and perfect, not a path of deprivation and difficulty.

How can you devote your life more to God?

Encouragement

The Lord your God is with you;
the mighty One will save you.
He will rejoice over you. You will rest in his love;
he will sing and be joyful about you.

Zephaniah 3:17 NCV

Encourage one another daily,
as long as it is called "Today."

Hebrews 3:13 NIV

Kind words are like honey—
sweet to the soul and healthy for the body.

Proverbs 16:24 NLT

Be joyful. Grow to maturity.
Encourage each other. Live in harmony and peace.
Then the God of love and peace will be with you.

2 Corinthians 13:11 NLT

I love your words of encouragement, God. What a beautiful thought it is that you express your delight in me with songs. Your words are like honey—sweet and nourishing. Help me to encourage others with kind words so your joy and peace can be theirs. Forgive me when my words are cold and disapproving, bringing discouragement. Set a guard over my mouth so I do not sin against you and others.

God, you made children to be open books—their opinions pop out unfiltered. Their honesty is a wonderful thing until it becomes hurtful and cruel. Give my grandchildren a sensitive conscience so they will not use their words to criticize or ridicule others. Help them to see that others need the same kindness and encouragement that they do. Set a guard over their mouths too, so they will not sin against you and others.

How can you encourage someone today?

Enthusiasm

Whatever you do, work heartily,
as for the Lord and not for men, knowing that from the
Lord you will receive the inheritance as your reward.
You are serving the Lord Christ.

Colossians 3:23–24 ESV

"When I discovered your words, I devoured them.
They are my joy and my heart's delight,
for I bear your name,
O Lord God of Heaven's Armies."

Jeremiah 15:16 NLT

Make the most of every opportunity.
Let your conversation be always full of grace.

Colossians 4:5–6 NIV

Thanks, God, for giving us a purpose to our labors. I know that working is a privilege and a responsibility, but sometimes it becomes tedious and exhausting. I see in your Word that my daily tasks are not meaningless; I am not just going through motions—I am serving you. Ahead of me is my inheritance; behind me is a job well done. Help me to remember I don't need to impress other people by what I do; I just need to please you. Today I choose joy and determine to work with enthusiasm.

Help my grandkids to understand that their parents are not assigning chores to make their lives miserable. Help them to accept their responsibilities obediently and with enthusiasm. Keep their parents diligent as they strive to teach a good work ethic; help them not to yield to complaining. Grow my grandkids into adults who work as unto you.

How can you show enthusiasm for the season you are in right now?

Eternity

We are citizens of heaven, where the Lord Jesus Christ lives. And we are eagerly waiting for him to return as our Savior.

PHILIPPIANS 3:20 NLT

"And if I go and prepare a place for you,
I will come back and take you to be with me
that you also may be where I am."

JOHN 14:3 NIV

That will happen in a flash, as quickly as you can wink an eye. It will happen at the blast of the last trumpet. Then the dead will be raised to live forever. And we will be changed.

1 CORINTHIANS 15:52 NIRV

Surely your goodness and love will be with me all my life,
and I will live in the house of the LORD forever.

PSALM 23:6 NCV

God, you created me for eternity; in fact, as a child of God I am already a citizen of heaven. I'm not built to last long on this earth, and as the years go by I feel the pull of heaven growing stronger. I'm not anxious to go because I want to be with the family you've given me, but honestly, the thought of what lies ahead is sweeter as time hastens along. One day you will call my name and I will be given my new eternal body and live in your presence forever. Thank you, Lord!

Help my grandkids to trust you as their Savior while they are young so they can spend their entire lives looking forward to an eternity with you. Keep them from wasting years wandering aimlessly—make them citizens of heaven now.

Can you view eternity with a hopeful, happy heart, fully trusting in a good God?

Excellence

Finally, my brothers and sisters,
always think about what is true.
Think about what is noble, right and pure.
Think about what is lovely and worthy of respect.
If anything is excellent or worthy of praise,
think about those kinds of things.

Philippians 4:8 NIRV

By his divine power, God has given us everything we need for living a godly life. We have received all of this by coming to know him, the one who called us to himself by means of his marvelous glory and excellence.

2 Peter 1:3 NLT

The answer is, if you eat or drink, or if you do anything, do it all for the glory of God.

1 Corinthians 10:31 NCV

Lord, I love how you instruct us so thoroughly in Christian living—even in how we think. You know we do best when we fill our minds with things true, noble, reputable, and pure. I want to live my life with excellence and I know the way I think affects my actions. You've given me everything I need to live a godly life—even the ability to focus on what is good and right.

Help my grandchildren, to do the same: to see the good in everything and be quick to see the positive in people. Would you give them the strength to let go of negative, critical thoughts and keep their minds from becoming the devil's playground? May their excellent thinking result in a godly life that brings glory to you.

What can you do to take every thought captive to the obedience of Christ?

Faith

Through Christ you have come to trust in God. And you have placed your faith and hope in God because he raised Christ from the dead and gave him great glory.

1 Peter 1:21 NLT

If you have faith as small as a mustard seed, it is enough. You can say to this mountain, 'Move from here to there.' And it will move. Nothing will be impossible for you."

Matthew 17:20 NIRV

The important thing is faith— the kind of faith that works through love.

Galatians 5:6 NCV

Faith is confidence in what we hope for and assurance about what we do not see.

Hebrews 11:1 NIV

Oh Lord, how I long for my faith to increase. You don't ask for much, just a tiny bit—as small as a mustard seed—and with that little speck, you do great and mighty things. So today, I ask for a seed of faith as I pray for the many needs before me. Give me confidence in knowing that what I am believing for will become a reality because nothing is impossible with you.

I pray for each of my grandchildren, that they would first put their trust in you as their Savior and then grow in their faith throughout their lives. Protect them from the enemy who would attempt to steal it away. When they struggle with doubts, help them remember your promises and put their hope in you.

What gives you faith and hope in Jesus?

Faithfulness

Your lovingkindness, O Lord, extends to the heavens,
Your faithfulness reaches to the skies.

Psalm 36:5 NASB

The Lord is faithful, who will establish you
and guard you from the evil one.

2 Thessalonians 3:3 NKJV

Lord, you are my God; I will exalt you and praise
your name, for in perfect faithfulness you have done
wonderful things, things planned long ago.

Isaiah 25:1 NIV

The word of the Lord is upright,
and all his work is done in faithfulness.

Psalm 33:4 ESV

How I praise you for your faithfulness today, God. As I look back over the years, I can testify to the wonderful things you have done for me—you have provided for me, strengthened and comforted me, forgiven and protected me. When I am unfaithful to you, you remain utterly and completely trustworthy. I am so grateful.

Show yourself faithful today to my grandkids. Guard them from the evil one; help them to be mindful that even though they sometimes fail you, you remain faithful to them. Help them to see you at work in their daily lives and to quickly recognize the hand of God even in the small things. Thank you that your faithfulness reaches to the skies!

How have you seen the faithfulness of God played out in your life?

Family

"Choose for yourselves this day whom you will serve…
as for me and my household, we will serve the LORD."

JOSHUA 24:15 NIV

Her children arise and call her blessed;
her husband also, and he praises her.

PROVERBS 31:28 NIV

For this reason I bow my knees before the Father,
from whom every family in heaven
and on earth derives its name.

EPHESIANS 3:14-15 NASB

Thank you, Lord, for the family you have given me—both the one I was born into and the one you created through me. Thank you for drawing other family members into your family. We have chosen to serve you and have never regretted that decision. Today I kneel before you with praise and thanksgiving for the privilege of being a part of your household.

I pray that my grandkids would make that same decision. May their commitment to you be so deep and genuine, that one day they would say with their own families, "As for me and my house, we will serve the Lord."

How can you treasure your family today?

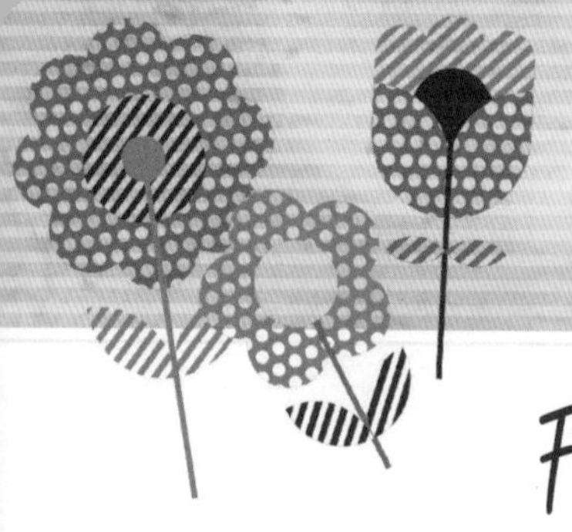

Fear

The Lord is my light and my salvation—
whom shall I fear?
The Lord is the stronghold of my life—
of whom shall I be afraid?

Psalm 27:1 NIV

We can say with confidence,
"The Lord is my helper, so I will have no fear.
What can mere people do to me?"

Hebrews 13:6 NLT

When I am afraid, I will trust you.
I praise God for his word.
I trust God, so I am not afraid.
What can human beings do to me?

Psalm 56:3-4 NCV

Thank you, Jesus, for the power I have through your Spirit to overcome fear. Fear has always been my primary opponent, and the best it has ever offered me is defeat and failure. I will continue to pray until my dying day, that you would help me resist the enemy, stand firm in my freedom, and let your promises become my strength. When I am afraid, help me trust in you. You are my light and salvation—whom shall I fear? What can man do to me?

I pray against a spirit of fear on behalf of my grandchildren. Remind their parents to guard what they see and experience so they are protected from needless attacks. When they are faced with a scary situation, help them to cry out to you for comfort and strength. I know your desire is that they grow into confident, courageous followers of the God who is the stronghold of their lives.

What fears can you give to God right now?

Forgiveness

"If you forgive other people when they sin against you,
your heavenly Father will also forgive you."

MATTHEW 6:14 NIV

Put up with each other. Forgive one another
if you are holding something against someone.
Forgive, just as the Lord forgave you.

COLOSSIANS 3:13 NIRV

God is faithful and fair. If we confess our sins, he will forgive our sins. He will forgive every wrong thing we have done. He will make us pure.

1 JOHN 1:9 NIRV

He is so rich in kindness and grace that he purchased our freedom with the blood of his Son and forgave our sins.

EPHESIANS 1:7 NLT

Search my heart today, God. Am I harboring unforgiveness or bitterness toward anyone? Sometimes I find myself retelling stories from years ago about someone who hurt me and the memory of it still has life. I don't want to carry around such baggage as I know if affects my relationship with you. How can you forgive me when I refuse to forgive and forget about the sins committed against me? I repent and let anyone who has offended me off the hook of my unforgiveness. You are so rich in kindness and grace—help me to extend the same to others.

I pray for my grandkids today. Please teach them how to be quick to forgive and quick to forget. They need to understand that if they don't forgive others for sinning against them, you cannot forgive them either. Fill them with grace that freely flows out to their friends and family.

Who might you need to extend forgiveness to today?

Friendship

A friend loves you all the time,
and a brother helps in time of trouble.

Proverbs 17:17 NCV

There are "friends" who destroy each other,
but a real friend sticks closer than a brother.

Proverbs 18:24 NLT

"Greater love has no one than this: to lay down one's life for one's friends. You are my friends if you do what I command.... Instead, I have called you friends, for everything that I learned from my Father I have made known to you."

John 15:13–15 NIV

"In everything, do to others
what you would want them to do to you."

Matthew 7:12 NIRV

Thank you for the gift of friendship. What a lonely life I would have without someone to share my life's experiences and deepest thoughts with. You are my friend because you have shared everything you learned from your Father with me. I am your friend if I follow your commands; help me to do that so our friendship can grow and deepen. I want to be a loving, faithful friend to others as well and treat them as I want to be treated. Thanks for being my friend!

Help my grandkids to develop good, godly friendships as they go through their growing up years. The wrong friends can destroy them; friends who set good examples by their attitudes and actions will help them to stay on track with you. Guard and protect their relationships, and help them stick close to you.

What friends spur you on in your relationship with God?

Generosity

Give generously to them and do so without a grudging heart; then because of this the LORD your God will bless you in all your work and in everything you put your hand to.

DEUTERONOMY 15:10 NIV

Each of you should give what you have decided in your heart to give. You shouldn't give if you don't want to. You shouldn't give because you are forced to. God loves a cheerful giver.

2 CORINTHIANS 9:7 NIRV

If you help the poor, you are lending to the LORD—and he will repay you!

PROVERBS 19:17 NLT

I understand, God, that I do not give to get. My giving must come from an open, generous heart that finds joy in doing so. Your generosity to me knows no limits—you own the cattle on a thousand hills, the wealth in every mine; yet, you find pleasure in meeting my needs. My resources are not unlimited, but you said that a widow's mite is more valuable to you than the treasures of the rich. I want to share what you've given me with a loving heart and open hands. Thank you for the blessings that always follow!

I pray earnestly today that my grandchildren will become people of generosity. The desire for money and things brings nothing but trouble. Save them from their own selfishness—make them big-hearted and open-handed. Help them to remember that when they help the poor, they are giving you a loan, which you will pay back in abundance.

How do you feel when you share with others?

Gentleness

"Accept my teachings and learn from me,
because I am gentle and humble in spirit,
and you will find rest for your lives."

MATTHEW 11:29 NCV

"Blessed are those who are humble.
They will be given the earth."

MATTHEW 5:5 NIRV

A gentle answer turns away wrath,
but a harsh word stirs up anger.

PROVERBS 15:1 NIV

Some people have gone astray without knowing it.
He is able to deal gently with them.
He can do that because he himself is weak.

HEBREWS 5:2 NIRV

When I hear the word gentle, I immediately think of a young mom cooing in soft tones to her infant, running her fingers over the velvety skin, treasuring the baby softness and sweet breath. No harsh tones, no roughness, no impatience, only warmth and tenderness. That's how you treat me, God. You are patient, kind, loving, and humble. I want to be like that too.

I've watched young toddlers delight in other babies. Their tender hugs and kisses are genuine, flowing from a heart full of love. I'm not asking that you remove the rough and tumble from their dispositions—only that you help them to be gentle with their words and actions to all the people in their lives Thank you, God.

What are some steps you can take to become more gentle?

Goodness

Everything God created is good, and nothing is to be rejected if it is received with thanksgiving.

1 TIMOTHY 4:4 NIV

Taste and see that the LORD is good.
Oh, the joys of those who take refuge in him!

PSALM 34:8 NLT

My brothers and sisters, I am sure that you are full of goodness. I know that you have all the knowledge you need and that you are able to teach each other.

ROMANS 15:14 NCV

God, you are good and your mercies endure forever! Thank you that there is refuge for me in that goodness, and there I find great joy. It's your goodness that leads me to repentance; it's because of your goodness that you provide for me, give me strength, and lead me in the way everlasting. You fill my life with good and perfect gifts.

I've said to my grandkids, "Be good now," but I know my words are powerless in themselves to change their behavior. Goodness comes from inside and is put there during the great spiritual exchange—when you remove our sin and fill us with your righteousness. I pray that my grandchildren would have that experience and would live lives of goodness and joy.

Where do you see the goodness of God the most in your life?

Grace

From his fullness we have all received,
grace upon grace.

John 1:16 NRSV

God gives us even more grace,
as the Scripture says, "God is against the proud,
but he gives grace to the humble."

James 4:6 NCV

Sin is no longer your master, for you no longer live
under the requirements of the law.
Instead, you live under the freedom of God's grace.

Romans 6:14 NLT

Heavenly Father, thank you for your limitless grace—from the moment you sent your only Son to this dark world to take on our sin, to this very day. I haven't done a thing to merit your favor, yet you extend it over and over again. I'm thinking about your servant David today, how he loved you with his whole heart, yet succumbed to his own lusts and did evil in your sight. He repented when confronted, and you restored to him the joy of his salvation. My heart is filled with gratitude for your grace upon grace.

I pray today that your grace would protect my grandkids from their own evil desires. Keep them from sin that would take them captive and destroy their lives. Give them a tender conscience and the desire to do your will. Help them to know that you aren't demanding perfection, just obedience and surrender to your will.

What does God's grace look like in your life?

Grief

Those who sow in tears shall reap with shouts of joy.

Psalm 126:5 ESV

Let your steadfast love become my comfort
according to your promise to your servant.

Psalm 119:76 NRSV

"Come to me, all you who are weary and burdened,
and I will give you rest. Take my yoke upon you
and learn from me, for I am gentle and humble in heart,
and you will find rest for your souls."

Matthew 11:28-29 NIV

Every valley shall be raised up,
every mountain and hill made low;
the rough ground shall become level,
the rugged places a plain.

Isaiah 40:4 NIV

My heart is heavy today, God. I am weary and burdened and sad. Loss is painful and there isn't a thing to do about it except to bring the burden to you. Only you can give rest for weariness and relief from the load of grief. Help me to accept your invitation to throw myself upon your shoulders and receive your comfort. One day, all the tears sown in sorrow will be wiped away, and I will reap a harvest of joy! Thank you for that beautiful promise.

When my grandchildren face sorrow, help them to turn to you, not away from you. The questions that come with seemingly meaningless tragedy can challenge even the strongest faith. Protect them from doubt. Shield them from the enemy who would use the opportunity to lure them away. Help them experience your presence, your peace, and your comfort.

Do you ask God for help when you need his comfort?

Guidance

Guide me in your truth and teach me,
for you are God my Savior,
and my hope is in you all day long.

Psalm 25:5 NIV

Wise people can also listen and learn;
even they can find good advice in these words.

Proverbs 1:5 NCV

We can make our plans,
but the Lord determines our steps.

Proverbs 16:9 NLT

Those who are led by the Spirit of God
are children of God.

Romans 8:14 NIRV

As you know, God, I am a terrible navigator; it's as though I was born directionless. I am grateful for technology that enables me to get from here to there almost effortlessly. But I am more thankful for your Word that leads and guides me on the path of life. Make me wise enough to listen and learn, and obedient enough to follow your plan. I am your child, and you have promised to instruct me in the way I should go.

Help my children to teach their kids to walk in your ways and guide them into all truth. Give my grandkids the desire to obey. For those children who have no one in their lives to train them in godliness, bring someone into their lives who can. Awaken a longing in their hearts for meaning and purpose, so they will not wander through life aimlessly.

Is there anything God can help guide you in today?

Guilt

God is faithful and fair. If we confess our sins,
he will forgive our sins.
He will forgive every wrong thing we have done.
He will make us pure.

1 John 1:9 NIRV

The Lord and King helps me. He won't let me be dishonored. So I've made up my mind to keep on serving him. I know he won't let me be put to shame.

Isaiah 50:7 NIRV

Those who go to him for help are happy,
and they are never disgraced.

Psalm 34:5 NCV

I have not achieved it, but I focus on this one thing:
Forgetting the past and looking forward to what lies ahead.

Philippians 3:13 NLT

Jesus, when you died for our sins you paid the penalty we deserved. You removed our transgressions and they are lost in the sea of your forgetfulness. Sometimes though, memories of my past sin resurface, and once again I feel the sting of regret. Then I remember that you have no recollection of these sins so it is pointless to rehash them. When I fail and need your grace once again, you are there to forgive and forget. Help me to forgive myself, forget the past, and look forward to all that lies ahead.

A guilty conscience weighs heavy on the heart until sin is confessed and the soul is washed clean. Give my grandchildren a tender conscience—make them quick to confess and repent—and quick to forgive themselves. Help them not to carry around needless guilt and to live in the freedom of forgiveness.

Why doesn't God want you to feel guilt and shame?

Health

The world and its desires pass away,
but whoever does the will of God lives forever.

1 John 2:17 NIV

Don't be wise in your own eyes.
Have respect for the Lord and avoid evil.
That will bring health to your body.
It will make your bones strong.

Proverbs 3:7-8 NIRV

I will never forget your commandments,
for by them you give me life.

Psalm 119:93 NLT

A happy heart is like good medicine,
but a broken spirit drains your strength.

Proverbs 17:22 NCV

Thank you, God, for the beautiful gift of life that will last for eternity. Sickness and death are realities in this fallen world, but your promises give us hope. You are the Great Physician, our wisdom, joy, and strength. I pray today that your healing power would minister to those I know who are ill, bringing health to their bodies and strength to their bones. I ask that my strength would remain all of my days, so I can complete my work on earth and finish strong.

Be near to my grandchildren in times of sickness. Help them not to be afraid but to trust in you. Heal them, give them life spiritually and physically, and fill their hearts with happiness.

What healing are you believing God for right now?

Helpfulness

"In everything I did, I showed you that by this kind of hard work we must help the weak, remembering the words the Lord Jesus himself said: 'It is more blessed to give than to receive.'"

ACTS 20:35 NIV

"Who is more important?
Is it the one at the table, or the one who serves?
Isn't it the one who is at the table?
But I am among you as one who serves."

LUKE 22:27 NIRV

Share with God's people who need help.
Bring strangers in need into your homes.

ROMANS 12:13 NCV

Helping others comes so naturally to some people, God. They can discern the need, whether physical or spiritual, and put a plan into action to meet that need. Sometimes a helping hand is appropriate, at other times it's a word of encouragement and affirmation through Scripture and prayer. I have often been the recipient of such kindness myself and I want to learn how to better extend that same mercy and grace to others.

Kids can be so selfish and consumed with themselves that it's easy for them to be unaware of someone else's needs. My grandkids are no different. Open their eyes, so they can see beyond themselves and notice a lonely classmate, or an untied shoe, or a grocery bag too heavy to carry. Help them to understand it really is more blessed to give than to receive.

What is something helpful you could do for someone today?

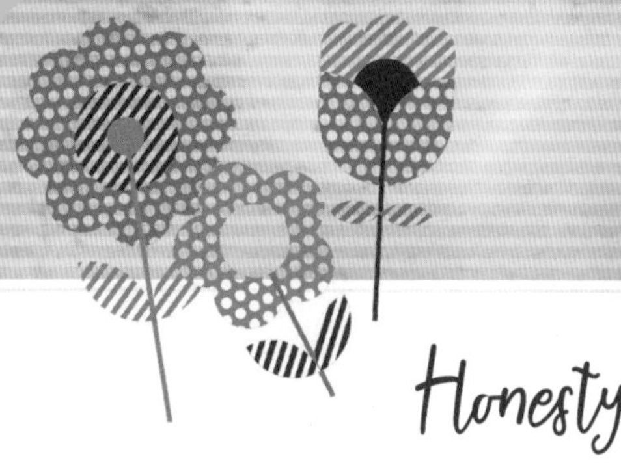

Honesty

Keep me from deceitful ways;
be gracious to me and teach me your law.
I have chosen the way of faithfulness;
I have set my heart on your laws.

PSALM 119:29–30 NIV

"Everything that is hidden will become clear,
and every secret thing will be made known."

LUKE 8:17 NCV

The king is pleased with words from righteous lips;
he loves those who speak honestly.

PROVERBS 16:13 NLT

Instead, we will speak the truth in love. So we will grow up in every way to become the body of Christ. Christ is the head of the body.

EPHESIANS 4:15 NIRV

Lord, you said in your Word that you detest lying lips—in fact, they are an abomination to you. I confess that sometimes to save face or avoid embarrassment, I tweak the truth just a bit with a half answer or purposely give an impression that isn't exactly accurate. I repent of this. I want my lips to speak honestly because I know that every secret thing will some day be made known and I want to please you by my words. Keep me from deceitful ways, and help me to walk in your truth.

Give my grandkids a sensitive conscience and a commitment to only speak truth. This means they will have to face the music from time to time, but give them the courage to be honest anyway. Trust is earned by honesty. May they grow into young men and women who are known for their integrity and trustworthiness.

Is there anything you need to be honest about now?

Hope

The LORD is good to those whose hope is in him,
to the one who seeks him.

LAMENTATIONS 3:25 NIV

Hope will never bring us shame. That's because God's love has poured into our hearts. This happened through the Holy Spirit, who has been given to us.

ROMANS 5:5 NIRV

The LORD's delight is in those who fear him,
those who put their hope in his unfailing love.

PSALM 147:11 NLT

Father, the hope that you give is what keeps us traveling on through all kinds of difficulties. Hope will never disappoint us. We await the blessed hope—the appearing of our Lord in the clouds when the living and the dead in Christ will be whisked away to live forever with you. Jesus, I choose today to put my hope in your unfailing love that never lets me down.

It's so sad to see children who are hopeless: lacking love, nourishment, and care. You love them and your heart is broken to see the effect sin has had on your precious creations. Spare them from suffering; send them someone who can bring them the hope that is in you. I pray today that you would use my grandchildren to minister to those who are hopeless and lost, and share the hope they have found in you.

Knowing that God always hears you, what can you be hopeful for?

Humility

"The people I value are not proud.
They are sorry for the wrong things they have done.
They have great respect for what I say."

Isaiah 66:2 NIRV

Humble yourselves before the Lord,
and he will lift you up.

James 4:10 NIV

Pride will ruin people,
but those who are humble will be honored.

Proverbs 29:23 NCV

The Lord has told you what is good,
and this is what he requires of you:
to do what is right, to love mercy,
and to walk humbly with your God.

Micah 6:8 NLT

There are great dichotomies in Jesus' teachings: to be strong, you must be weak; to be rich you must become poor; to be first you must be last; to lead you must serve; to be lifted up you must humble yourself. I love how your ways just do not fit in with our human way of thinking. Today I humble myself before you, realizing again how helpless I am without you. When pride raises its ugly head, remind me that nothing worthwhile is accomplished in my life without the grace and strength of your Holy Spirit.

There is a fine balance between confidence and arrogance—children especially do not know how to differentiate between the two. I want my grandkids to be self-confident and unafraid, but not to the point of conceit. Help them, Jesus, to be confident in who you have made them to be, but not boastful.

What opportunities might give you a chance to practice humility today?

Inspiration

The precepts of the LORD are right,
giving joy to the heart.
The commands of the LORD are radiant,
giving light to the eyes.

PSALM 19:8 NIV

Your laws are my treasure;
they are my heart's delight.

PSALM 119:111 NLT

The whole Bible was given to us by inspiration from God and is useful to teach us what is true and to make us realize what is wrong in our lives; it straightens us out and helps us do what is right.

2 TIMOTHY 3:16 TLB

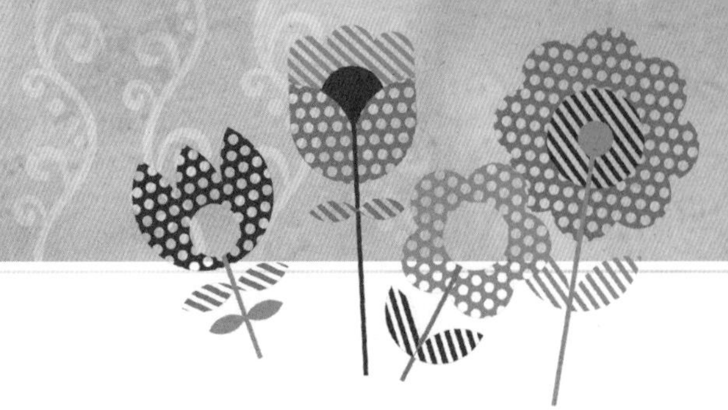

God, I am so thankful for your inspired Word that teaches us truth, guides our decisions, and gives us the motivation we need to follow you wholeheartedly. We don't have to wander aimlessly throughout life without a road map and a guide. Often I lack the enthusiasm for life; I feel flat and uninspired. Even reading your Word sounds ho-hum at times, and I'd rather take a nap. I know your precepts bring joy; your commandments shine like the stars, illuminating our path. Help me to delight in your Word, inspire me by it; make it my treasure.

May my grandchildren's dreams be inspired by you. Give them a love for your Word. May it settle deep in their hearts and be the inspiration for all they do in their lives. Give them a desire to seek after truth and to serve others.

How do you find inspiration?

Integrity

I know, my God, that you test the heart and are pleased with integrity. All these things I have given willingly and with honest intent.

1 Chronicles 29:17 NIV

"So if you ignore the least commandment and teach others to do the same, you will be called the least in the Kingdom of Heaven. But anyone who obeys God's laws and teaches them will be called great in the Kingdom of Heaven."

Matthew 5:19 NLT

The honest person will live in safety,
but the dishonest will be caught.

Proverbs 10:9 NCV

God, my desire is to be a woman of integrity. I want to be someone with unwavering and uncompromising convictions, yet be able to speak the truth in love. I want to be the real deal—the same inside and outside of church—reliable, trustworthy, honest, and sincere. When I do a good deed, may it be willingly and with pure motives and no hidden agendas. When you test my heart, I want you to be pleased.

Father, I pray that you would help my grandkids to be honest and forthright. Keep them from yielding to the temptation to hide the truth to avoid consequences. May they grow into adults who are honest in all their dealings and who obey your laws so they can teach others the same.

Do you admire the integrity of someone in your life?

Joy

May the God of hope fill you with all joy and peace
as you trust in him, so that you may overflow with hope
by the power of the Holy Spirit.

ROMANS 15:13 NIV

"Don't be sad, because the joy of the LORD
will make you strong."

NEHEMIAH 8:10 NCV

The LORD is my strength and shield.
I trust him with all my heart.
He helps me, and my heart is filled with joy.
I burst out in songs of thanksgiving.

PSALM 28:7 NLT

Always be joyful because you belong to the Lord.
I will say it again. Be joyful!

PHILIPPIANS 4:4 NIRV

God, it sounds to me like you're telling me to choose joy. That's a difficult concept, especially when things aren't going very well. In Romans, you say that joy comes from you and that it will make me strong. I see in Philippians that I am to be joyful just because I belong to you. You don't say anything about the circumstances. So today, I choose joy! I'll put it on like a garment and wear it all day long. Actually, I feel a song of thanksgiving coming on—praise be to the God who fills my heart with joy and peace!

Help my grandkids not to allow themselves to be grumpy when things don't go exactly their way. I sometimes do the same thing, but by this time in my life, I've learned a bit of self-control. Teach them how to see the good and positive things around them and to be filled with thanksgiving. Help them to choose joy.

What is one truly joyful moment you've had recently?

Justice

My friends, do not try to punish others when they wrong you, but wait for God to punish them with his anger. It is written: "I will punish those who do wrong; I will repay them," says the Lord.

Romans 12:19 NCV

He is the Rock. His works are perfect.
All his ways are right. He is faithful.
He doesn't do anything wrong. He is honest and fair.

Deuteronomy 32:4 NIRV

The Lord secures justice for the poor
and upholds the cause of the needy.

Psalm 140:12 NIV

There is joy for those who deal justly with others
and always do what is right.

Psalm 106:3 NLT

Heavenly Father, thank you that you are a God of justice. When somebody wrongs me, I don't have to worry about revenge. You punish those who sin against me—it's not my job to do that. You are honest and fair; you go to bat for the poor and needy. You offer joy to those who deal fairly with others and always do what is right. I pray that you would help me deal justly with my family and grandkids. I don't want to show favoritism or be unfair in any way.

Help my grandkids not to retaliate when they are wronged. It is their inclination as it is mine. When they are angry, give them self-control. When others hurt or offend them, help them to wait for you to punish the offender. Help them to treat their friends and siblings fairly and may they find joy in doing what is right.

Why is it better to let God be the judge?

Kindness

Be kind to each other, tenderhearted, forgiving one another, just as God through Christ has forgiven you.

Ephesians 4:32 NLT

Kind people do themselves a favor,
but cruel people bring trouble on themselves.

Proverbs 11:17 NCV

Do you disrespect God's great kindness and favor?
Do you disrespect God when he is patient with you?
Don't you realize that God's kindness
is meant to turn you away from your sins?

Romans 2:4 NIRV

For great is his love toward us,
and the faithfulness of the Lord endures forever.
Praise the Lord.

Psalm 117:2 NIV

God, I know people who are defined by kindness. They are tenderhearted, gentle, patient, and forgiving. I haven't heard harsh words come out of their mouths. I want to be like that. I want to be quick to listen, slow to speak, and slow to get angry—and yes, quick to forgive. It's because of your kindness that I am forgiven and destined for heaven. Draw others to you through my kindness and lead them to repentance.

My grandma heart is so pleased when I hear kind words spoken: "Can I help? Are you okay? Here's a toy you can play with." When a little one willingly lends a hand to another without complaining, I know the awesome love of God is at work. Grow them into people of kindness.

How can you extend kindness to those around you today?

Loneliness

"Teach them to obey everything that I have taught you,
and I will be with you always,
even until the end of this age."

Matthew 28:20 NCV

The Lord is near to all who call on him,
yes, to all who call on him in truth.

Psalm 145:18 NLT

Even if my father and mother abandon me,
the Lord will hold me close.

Psalm 27:10 NLT

"Be strong and courageous. Do not be afraid or terrified
because of them, for the Lord your God goes with you;
he will never leave you nor forsake you."

Deuteronomy 31:6 NIV

Lord, thank you that your presence is constantly with me. You reveal yourself to me through a moving song; I feel your presence around me in the beauty of creation; I see your smile on the face of a passerby. Most of all, your presence is revealed in my heart—the peace I experience, the joy even when I am alone, and the sustaining hope of eternal life. When I am forlorn and missing a loved one, remind me to reach out to someone else who is lonely and needs your comfort.

You created us with the desire to belong—to fit in. Friends get more and more important to children as the years go by, but even in a crowd it's possible for them to feel lonely. Loneliness is real. Help my grandkids to remember that you are there with them at all times and in all places; they will never be abandoned.

When you feel lonely, can you turn to God and ask him to surround you with his presence?

Love

Three things will last forever—
faith, hope, and love—
and the greatest of these is love.

1 Corinthians 13:13 NLT

Lord, you are good. You are forgiving.
You are full of love for all who call out to you.

Psalm 86:5 NIRV

Fill us with your love every morning.
Then we will sing and rejoice all our lives.

Psalm 90:14 NCV

Let love and faithfulness never leave you;
bind them around your neck,
write them on the tablet of your heart.

Proverbs 3:3 NIV

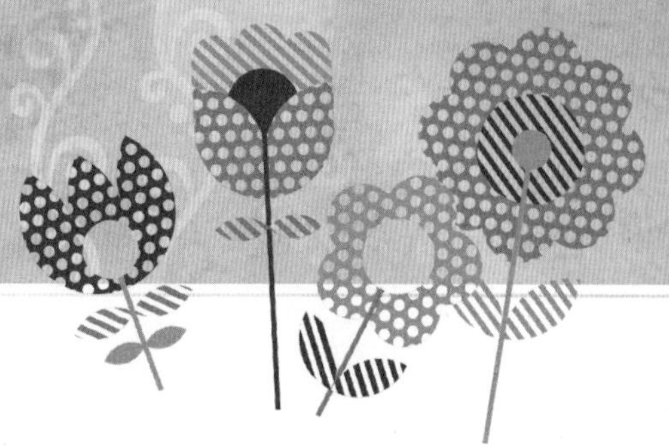

I often find myself singing, "The steadfast love of the Lord never ceases, your mercies never come to an end. They are new every morning, new every morning. Great is your faithfulness, O Lord." Thank you that your love covers all of my sins and shortcomings every day, and I can start each day with a clean slate. Build my faith as I spend time in your Word. Keep hope alive and growing, but most of all, pour out your love in my heart so it can overflow to others.

I pray that my grandchildren would experience the great love you have for them. Help them to recognize that all the good things in their lives are ultimately from your hand. Their health, friends, parents, provision, and shelter are all evidences of your love for them. Open their young eyes so they can see you.

How does the love of God in your life help you to love others?

Patience

Warn those who are lazy. Encourage those who are timid.
Take tender care of those who are weak.
Be patient with everyone.

1 THESSALONIANS 5:14 NLT

Be like those who through faith and patience
will receive what God has promised.

HEBREWS 6:12 NCV

Be completely humble and gentle;
be patient, bearing with one another in love.

EPHESIANS 4:2 NIV

Anyone who is patient has great understanding.
But anyone who gets angry quickly
shows how foolish they are.

PROVERBS 14:29 NIRV

Heavenly Father, how I wish there was a way to develop patience without it being tested! Any patience that I do have is the result of suffering you have allowed in my life. You used it to expand my capacity to endure. The patience I need on a day-to-day basis is where I need the most help—it's the little things that get to me. Continue your work in my life. Help me be patient with those who irritate me and in situations that get under my skin.

The unsanctified little lives that I love so much are usually short on patience. Many could be considered "high need" because immediately upon entering the room, the demands commence! "Can I have...? Will you help me with...? I'm hungry! How come I can't...?" Jesus, help my grandkids in this area. Give them large doses of patience that they don't even know how to ask for.

How can you show more patience in your life?

Peace

"I have told you these things, so that you can have peace because of me. In this world you will have trouble. But be encouraged! I have won the battle over the world."

John 16:33 NIRV

The Lord gives his people strength.
The Lord blesses them with peace.

Psalm 29:11 NLT

May the Lord of peace himself give you peace at all times and in every way. The Lord be with all of you.

2 Thessalonians 3:16 NIV

"I am leaving you with a gift—peace of mind and heart. And the peace I give is a gift the world cannot give. So don't be troubled or afraid."

John 14:27 NLT

God, there's just nothing like having peace of mind and heart. I praise your name today for that gift—one that the world cannot give. You are the only source of peace. It doesn't magically come only when everything is going perfectly. Inner turmoil can be present no matter the circumstances. Thank you for delivering me time and time again from anxiety and fear when peace had eluded me. Help me to let your peace always reign in my heart and keep me from allowing the enemy to steal it away.

Sometimes my grandkids are anxious—whether it's from a significant change in plans, a new situation, or a doctor's visit—their anxieties are very real. I pray that you would give them peace in their hearts during scary times. Help them to remember that you are always with them and can take away their fears.

What does peace look like for you?

Perseverance

In a race all the runners run. But only one gets the prize.
You know that, don't you?
So run in a way that will get you the prize.

1 CORINTHIANS 9:24–25 NIRV

I have tried hard to find you—
don't let me wander from your commands.

PSALM 119:10 NLT

I have fought the good fight,
I have finished the race,
I have kept the faith.

2 TIMOTHY 4:7 NCV

Let us not become weary in doing good,
for at the proper time we will reap a harvest
if we do not give up.

GALATIANS 6:9 NIV

God, some people put their hand to the plow and never turn back. It is in their nature to persevere, as though you instilled it in their DNA. Others struggle to keep focused on a task and get easily sidetracked, procrastinating their plans away. Why do most of us fall in the second arena in our devotional and prayer life, where perseverance is most vital? Often my over-active mind and busy ways distract me. Help me persevere so I can perfect my faith and finish the race strong!

Don't you get a kick out of how your little ones can fiddle around and turn a very easy task into a long, laborious undertaking? I can laugh at my grandkids now, but it wasn't so funny when my own were little. Teach these precious ones how to persevere, and please make the lessons they need to learn as painless as possible! Give their parents perseverance in training them.

What do you feel God is calling you to persevere in right now?

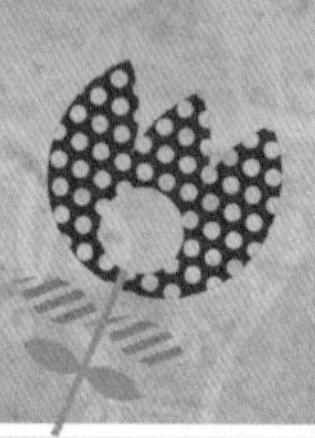

Praise

Sing to the Lord a new song,
his praise from the ends of the earth,
you who go down to the sea, and all that is in it,
you islands, and all who live in them.

Isaiah 42:10 NIV

Praise the Lord from the skies.
Praise him high above the earth.
Praise him, all you angels.
Praise him, all you armies of heaven.
Praise him, sun and moon.
Praise him, all you shining stars.
Praise him, highest heavens
and you waters above the sky.
Let them praise the Lord,
because they were created by his command.

Psalm 148:1-5 NCV

Oh Father, I praise your wonderful name today! I raise my hands and my heart to you as I meditate on your sacrificial love, the forgiveness and salvation you offer, and your transforming love. I join my praise with millions of your saints on earth and angels in heaven at this moment. Praise you for choosing us to be your people; praise you that you made us royal priests and we are your special treasure. Thank you for bringing us out of darkness into your wonderful light. There is none like you, God.

Please instill a love in my grandchildren's hearts for praise and worship. I pray that they would enter in wholeheartedly to the songs and prayers being led. Help them to experience your presence as they sing—quicken their spirits and let them know you are real and worthy to be praised.

What is something specific you can praise God for today?

Prayer

Lord, in the morning you hear my voice.
In the morning I pray to you. I wait for you in hope.

Psalm 5:3 NIRV

Never stop praying.

1 Thessalonians 5:17 NIRV

The Lord does not listen to the wicked,
but he hears the prayers of those who do right.

Proverbs 15:29 NCV

Come, let us bow down in worship,
let us kneel before the Lord our Maker.

Psalm 95:6 NIV

What a privilege to have instant access to the Creator of the universe. God, you tell us that instead of worrying about anything, we should pray. When we are sick, we should pray. When we are rejoicing in a victory won, we are to pray. Forgive me for not taking enough time to talk to you. You want to be a participant in my life; in fact, you want to be in charge of my life. Help me never to neglect our relationship.

Don't you love how kids pray? So simple, short, straightforward, and to the point. They speak from their hearts with no extra fluff. I'm sure you laugh with me at some of their requests! Help my grandkids to turn to you first with all of their needs and be slow to fret and quick to pray.

What can you pray about right now?

Protection

My God is my rock. I can run to him for safety.
He is my shield and my saving strength,
my defender and my place of safety.
The LORD saves me from those who want to harm me.

2 SAMUEL 22:3 NCV

The LORD keeps you from all harm
and watches over your life.
The LORD keeps watch over you as you come and go,
both now and forever.

PSALM 121:7-8 NLT

The LORD is good, a refuge in times of trouble.
He cares for those who trust in him.

NAHUM 1:7 NIV

Father, you are my rock, my shield, my defender, and my place of safety. In a world where your people are being increasingly persecuted for their faith, I can trust you to keep me safe from those who want to harm me. Keep my faith strong and be my defense in times of adversity. Protect my mind so I will not be deceived by the devil's lies. Protect me emotionally so I am not overcome by life's troubles. Protect me physically from disease and accidents. Thank you for keeping watch over me as I come and go.

God, please protect my grandchildren from evil. Insulate them from the wickedness of the culture—surround them with songs of deliverance. Keep them healthy mind, body, and emotions. Be their hiding place. I trust them into your care today.

How hard is it for you to lay down your battle plan and let God be your protector?

Purpose

You have been raised up with Christ.
So think about things that are in heaven.
That is where Christ is.
He is sitting at God's right hand.

Colossians 3:1 NIRV

We know that in all things God works
for the good of those who love him,
who have been called according to his purpose.

Romans 8:28 NIV

My child, pay attention to my words;
listen closely to what I say.
Don't ever forget my words;
keep them always in mind.

Proverbs 4:20–21 NCV

God, when I was a young mom, I wanted so much to do something extraordinary for you. I was raising little ones but somehow felt I needed to do more. You encouraged me that raising those children was "more." I am so grateful that you clarified my purpose. Mothering was enough—that was the big thing I thought had eluded me. Now I'm a grandma, loving on my precious grandchildren. You've given me different things to do, but they don't need to be impressive. It's enough to live and love those around me.

I pray that my grandkids would some day understand that your purpose for their lives is to love and follow you. You have gifted them uniquely. Help them to seek your guidance in how you want them to use their talents in daily life. May the passion of their lives be to glorify you.

How would you define God's purpose for your life?

Relationships

Two are better than one,
because they have a good return for their labor:
If either of them falls down,
one can help the other up.

ECCLESIASTES 4:9–10 NIV

Perfume and incense bring joy to the heart,
and the pleasantness of a friend
springs from their heartfelt advice.

PROVERBS 27:9 NIV

Love each other with genuine affection,
and take delight in honoring each other.

ROMANS 12:10 NLT

Thank you for the relationships you have brought into my life through the years. You designed us for fellowship, so you put us into families where we would not be alone or lost. I pray a blessing today on my loved ones. Continue to provide for their needs, comfort them when they are sad, direct them in the way they should go. Give us the grace to extend forgiveness and mercy to each other when needed. Help me to do my part in keeping each relationship alive. Give me a nudge when I need to call or lend a hand or pray.

I pray that you would protect my grandchildren from wrong relationships—from peers who are not a good influence—from anyone who might steer them in the wrong direction. Give them good friends to be with and teach them how to be a good friend to others.

Think of some of your closest relationships now and thank God for them.

Reliability

"All people are like grass. All their glory is like the flowers in the field. The grass dries up. The flowers fall to the ground. But the word of the LORD lasts forever."

1 PETER 1:24-25 NIRV

Every good action and every perfect gift is from God. These good gifts come down from the Creator of the sun, moon, and stars, who does not change like their shifting shadows.

JAMES 1:17 NCV

You are near, LORD,
and all your commands are true.
Long ago I learned from your statutes
that you established them to last forever.

PSALM 119:151-152 NIV

Thank you, Jesus, that I can count on you. There is a constancy about you that is comforting. Everything in my life keeps shifting and adjusting to the passage of time, except for you. Your Word lasts forever; you do not waver or vacillate like a shifting shadow. You do not forget your promises to me; you are not fickle and unreliable. You can be trusted. Make me the kind of person who is true to my word, who follows through with my intentions, and can always be counted on.

Teach my grandchildren to keep their word. Don't let them grow up to be flighty and unstable people who follow their own selfish whims. Help them to follow through on the promises they make, lest they become an irritant to others by their unreliability. May their example of integrity bring honor to your name.

How does it make you feel to know you can rely on God for everything?

Respect

Show respect for all people:
Love the brothers and sisters of God's family,
respect God, honor the king.

1 PETER 2:17 NCV

Trust in your leaders. Put yourselves under their authority. Do this, because they keep watch over you. They know they are accountable to God for everything they do. Do this, so that their work will be a joy. If you make their work a heavy load, it won't do you any good.

HEBREWS 13:17 NIRV

Acknowledge those who work hard among you, who care for you in the Lord and who admonish you. Hold them in the highest regard in love because of their work. Live in peace with each other.

1 THESSALONIANS 5:12-13 NIV

Father, I am convicted today by these verses. I do not naturally or easily submit to those over me or put my trust in them. I tend to see the negative and rather than humbly acknowledging their position and bringing any concerns to you, I feel obliged to share my observations with others. This is not the attitude you desire and definitely does not show respect. Yes, at times leaders fail, but they are accountable to you—not me. I choose today to put myself under authority, understanding that as I do, I am placing myself under your umbrella of protection.

I know that respectfully submitting to authority is a learned behavior. Help my children to teach this faithfully to my grandkids by word and example, that as they grow, they will naturally show respect to others.

How do you show respect to the authority figures in your life?

Reward

Work willingly at whatever you do, as though you were working for the Lord rather than for people. Remember that the Lord will give you an inheritance as your reward, and that the Master you are serving is Christ.

Colossians 3:23–24 NLT

"Love your enemies, do good to them, and lend to them without expecting to get anything back. Then your reward will be great, and you will be children of the Most High, because he is kind to the ungrateful and wicked."

Luke 6:35 NIV

Without faith it is impossible to please God. Those who come to God must believe that he exists. And they must believe that he rewards those who look to him.

Hebrews 11:6 NIRV

God, I honestly don't think about getting rewards from you very often. I do think about heaven quite a bit because I have so many loved ones there now. What does it mean to work heartily for you so you will give us an inheritance? Are you talking about heaven or about a reward in the here and now? I think it's both: my reward is the joy of knowing you now and the ultimate joy of being in your presence forever in heaven. In both cases, the reward is joy! Thank you so much for this simple, yet profound word to my heart today.

My grandkids love to be rewarded for a job well done or at least the promise of a reward certainly motivates them to get a move on! Help them to experience your joy when they obey and help them to understand that when they are doing their chores, they are really doing them for you.

How does it make you feel knowing that God is rewarding you for your diligence?

Salvation

"This is how God loved the world: He gave his one and only Son, so that everyone who believes in him will not perish but have eternal life."

John 3:16 NLT

The wages of sin is death,
but the gift of God is eternal life in Christ Jesus our Lord.

Romans 6:23 NIV

God's grace has saved you because of your faith in Christ.
Your salvation doesn't come from anything you do.
It is God's gift.

Ephesians 2:8 NIRV

If you openly declare that Jesus is Lord and believe in your heart that God raised him from the dead, you will be saved.

Romans 10:9 NLT

God, I know you remember the moment I gave my heart to you. When I cried out to you, I felt a light go on inside of me. I know now that your Holy Spirit entered my heart at that very moment and I became your child. I will never forget it or cease to be grateful. Thank you for saving me from my sin and giving me the gift of eternal life.

I pray that all my grandchildren will receive you as their personal Savior. Help them to understand that their sin separates them from you and that you died for them—you took the punishment they deserve. Open their hearts to believe and receive. Shine your light of salvation in their hearts.

How do you respond to the message of salvation?

Serving

Each of you should use whatever gift you have received to serve others, as faithful stewards of God's grace in its various forms. If anyone serves, they should do so with the strength God provides, so that in all things God may be praised through Jesus Christ.

1 Peter 4:10-11 NIV

Always give yourselves fully to the work of the Lord, because you know that your labor in the Lord is not in vain.

1 Corinthians 15:58 NIV

You were called to freedom…
do not use your freedom as an opportunity for the flesh,
but through love serve one another.

Galatians 5:13 ESV

Thanks for the privilege of serving you, God, and for the strength you provide to do it. It is a privilege to be your hands and feet to the world because we know that anything we do for others is never a waste of time. You have equipped each of us with a tool set suited for specific tasks. Help me to give myself fully in the area I am to serve and to do so motivated by love and enthusiasm. Help me never to tire of going good.

Teach my grandkids what a blessing it is to serve others. We live in a very self-focused culture where personal happiness seems to be everyone's goal. Help them turn their eyes outward and see the needs around them. Give them joy in doing for others.

Is there a way you can serve God and your grandchildren today?

Strength

God is our refuge and strength,
an ever-present help in trouble.

Psalm 46:1-3 NIV

The Lord is faithful;
he will strengthen you and guard you from the evil one.

2 Thessalonians 3:3 NIRV

Don't be afraid, for I am with you.
Don't be discouraged, for I am your God.
I will strengthen you and help you.
I will hold you up with my victorious right hand.

Isaiah 41:10 NLT

God, I have cried out to you for strength so many times throughout my life, for help in times of trouble, for protection from the evil one. Thank you for answering these prayers and being exactly the God you promise to be. Your grace is all I need, and your power is made known through my shortcomings. Sometimes I resent my weakness, but right now I thank you for it because only in it can I experience your miraculous strength.

Be with my grandkids wherever they are—at school, home, with friends, or in church. Help them not to be afraid or discouraged but to hold to your victorious right hand. Help them to know you as their faithful, strong, ever-present God!

What is your source of strength?

Stress

Praise the Lord, my soul;
all my inmost being, praise his holy name.
Praise the Lord, my soul,
and forget not all his benefits—
who forgives all your sins
and heals all your diseases,
who redeems your life from the pit
and crowns you with love and compassion,
who satisfies your desires with good things
so that your youth is renewed like the eagle's.

Psalm 103:1-5 NIV

Commit your actions to the Lord.
and your plans will succeed.

Proverbs 16:3 NLT

When I read Psalm 103, God, I have to wonder why I ever feel overwhelmed! If I concentrated on all your marvelous benefits, I would be at rest all the time. You forgive my sins, heal my sicknesses, deliver me from the enemy, fill me with your love and compassion, and satisfy my desires. On top of that, you give me back my youth when I'm in your presence. Help me to experience all your benefits and let your peace dwell in my heart.

Children feel stress for a variety of reasons. When they have too much homework, God, be their wisdom; when there is sickness or conflict, be their healer; when they are just too busy, save them from discouragement. Please give their parents wisdom as they prioritize activities. I ask that peace would reign in my grandchildren's hearts and in their homes.

When was the last time you were able to let go of stress and just sit with God?

Teaching

All scripture is inspired by God and is useful for teaching, for reproof, for correction, and for training in righteousness, so that everyone who belongs to God may be proficient, equipped for every good work.

2 Timothy 3:16–17 NRSV

Let each generation tell its children of your mighty acts; let them proclaim your power.

Psalm 145:4 NLT

"Go therefore and make disciples of all the nations, baptizing them in the name of the Father and of the Son and of the Holy Spirit, teaching them to observe all things that I have commanded you."

Matthew 28:19–20 NKJV

God, some say that lessons are more caught than taught. But I see in your Word that teaching is more than being an example; it is expressed in words. You've given us Scripture that trains, teaches, reproves, corrects, and trains us in righteousness. Then you tell us to teach others all that we've learned. Help me to be faithful in transmitting your mighty works in my life to the next generation.

I pray that my grandchildren would have teachable spirits. Give them open hearts to receive your truth and a willingness to respond to correction. Help them to respect the teachers in their lives—at school, at church, and at home—so they can grow in righteousness.

When is it easiest to teach your grandchildren about God?

Thankfulness

I have not stopped giving thanks for you,
remembering you in my prayers.
EPHESIANS 1:16 NIV

Giving thanks is a sacrifice that truly honors me.
If you keep to my path,
I will reveal to you the salvation of God.
PSALM 50:23 NLT

Rejoice always, pray continually,
give thanks in all circumstances;
for this is God's will for you in Christ Jesus.
1 THESSALONIANS 5:16–18 NIV

Give thanks as you enter the gates of his temple.
Give praise as you enter its courtyards.
Give thanks to him and praise his name.
PSALM 100:4 NIRV

God, I know you don't need my constant expression of thanksgiving, but I need it! An attitude of gratitude places you at the center of every circumstance. I can choose to rejoice; I can choose to give thanks even though it may be a sacrifice; I can choose to praise you continually. This is your will for me. Today I thank you for your many blessings; I praise you for freedom from sin and guilt; I praise you for provision, your presence, and your infinite love for me. Thank you for the eternal home that you have prepared for me that I will enjoy forever.

Teach my grandchildren to be thankful for what they have rather than wanting more. May their gratitude be genuine. You have blessed them above and beyond what we would ever have asked for and I pray they wouldn't take those things for granted. Fill their hearts to overflowing with appreciation for the abundance they enjoy.

What can you thank God for right now?

Trust

Those who know the LORD trust him,
because he will not leave those who come to him.

PSALM 9:10 NCV

I trust in you, LORD. I say, "You are my God."
My whole life is in your hands.
Save me from the hands of my enemies.
Save me from those who are chasing me.

PSALM 31:14-15 NIV

Yes, the LORD is for me; he will help me.
I will look in triumph at those who hate me.
It is better to take refuge in the LORD
than to trust in people.

PSALM 118:7-8 NLT

God, you have completely and overwhelmingly earned my trust. You have been faithful to me time and time again throughout my life. Even when I doubted your goodness, you didn't turn away; you just patiently waited for me to surrender. When I wondered if you even cared or heard my prayers, you remained constant. When I was ready to kneel once again at your throne of grace, you welcomed me back. I trust in you. You are my God. My future is in your hands.

Show my grandchildren that you are trustworthy. Answer their prayers from the smallest of requests to the biggest. Thank you for small miracles that increase their faith. Allow my grandkids to continue to witness your miracle-working power!

How do you know that God is trustworthy?

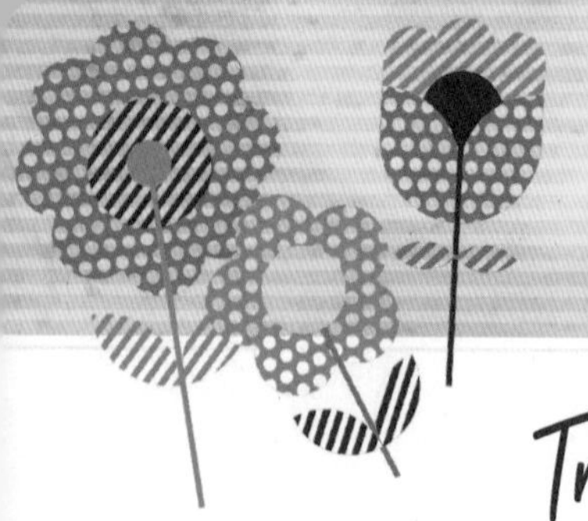

Truth

"When he, the Spirit of truth, comes,
he will guide you into all the truth."

John 16:13 NIV

The very essence of your words is truth;
all your just regulations will stand forever.

Psalm 119:160 NLT

"If you abide in My word,
you are My disciples indeed.
And you shall know the truth,
and the truth shall make you free."

John 8:31-32 NKJV

Teach me your way, O Lord, that I may walk in your truth;
unite my heart to fear your name.

Psalm 86:11 ESV

God, in a world where nothing is for sure, your Word is a bastion of truth that has stood the test of time. It is unchanging and unmovable; it guides my choices and leads me in the way I should go. It is absolute and freeing. Praise you for your truth that has set me free from sin, bondage, and darkness. It is my roadmap for life. Help me to walk in your truth all the days of my life.

I pray that my grandchildren will walk in your truth all of their lives as well. Shield them from the lies of the enemy that would steal them away and destroy them. May they be so convinced of your truth that the enemy's designs against them would fail. Hold them fast in your truth and by it set them free.

What steps can you take to be more truthful in your everyday life?

Understanding

Understanding is like a fountain of life
to those who have it.
But foolish people are punished
for the foolish things they do.

PROVERBS 16:22 NIRV

The teaching of your word gives light,
so even the simple can understand.

PSALM 119:130 NLT

Give me understanding,
so that I may keep your law
and obey it with all my heart.

PSALM 119:34 NIV

Don't act thoughtlessly,
but understand what the Lord wants you to do.

EPHESIANS 5:17 NLT

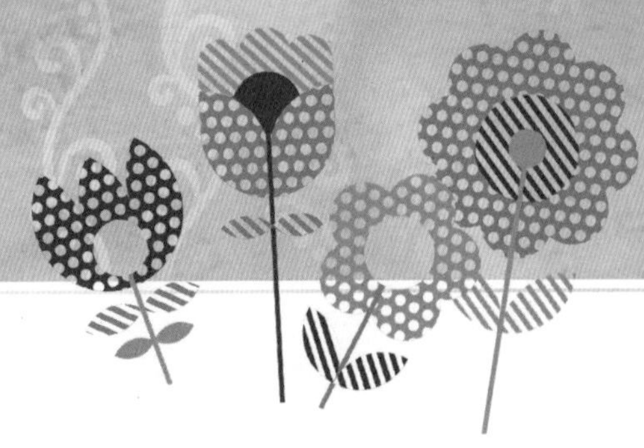

God, I need a greater depth of understanding when I read your Word. You wrote the Bible for the ordinary person, yet the Holy Spirit must quicken it to my soul—only then does it make sense. Please open the eyes of my heart to discover your unsearchable riches. Increase my comprehension. Give me spiritual discernment that exceeds my intelligence! Reveal your words to me so the light shines out and I can understand and obey it.

Help my grandkids understand that your ways are the best, and that your Word is a treasure chest waiting to be discovered. Give them a desire to search the Scriptures for hidden nuggets and then give them understanding to apply them.

How do you seek to understand God's will each day?

Victory

You can prepare a horse for the day of battle.
But the power to win comes from the LORD.

PROVERBS 21:31 NIRV

Every child of God defeats this evil world,
and we achieve this victory through our faith.

1 JOHN 5:4 NLT

From the LORD comes deliverance.
May your blessing be on your people.

PSALM 3:8 NIV

"The LORD your God is the one who goes with you to fight for you against your enemies to give you victory."

DEUTERONOMY 20:4 NIV

Praise you, God, that the battle against the enemy is fought and won by your power. Satan is no match for you because he was defeated on Calvary. Sometimes I forget that everything that comes against me is not just an unfortunate coincidence or a random misfortune on a lateral level. My struggle is not against flesh and blood but against the powers of this dark world. Remind me to put on the armor you have provided, stand on your promises, and let you do battle.

God, protect my grandkids from the attacks of the enemy. Keep them from discouragement and deliver them from the desire to retaliate when someone sins again them. Help them take every difficulty to you in prayer. Teach them that the Word of God is their defense and shield. They may be too young to understand spiritual warfare, but help them trust you in every situation.

You win with Jesus in your life! Can you think of the last victory you experienced?

Wisdom

Wisdom will come into your mind,
and knowledge will be pleasing to you.
Good sense will protect you;
understanding will guard you
It will keep you from the wicked,
from those whose words are bad.

PROVERBS 2:10-12 NCV

Wisdom and money can get you almost anything,
but only wisdom can save your life.

ECCLESIASTES 7:12 NLT

If any of you needs wisdom,
you should ask God for it.
He will give it to you.
God gives freely to everyone and doesn't find fault.

JAMES 1:5 NIRV

God, I need wisdom on a daily basis. There are so many decisions to make, some big, some small, but all need your guidance. I have made some wrong choices in my lifetime because I did not acknowledge your will in the matter. Thanks for your forgiveness. Thank you for allowing me to come to you and ask for wisdom—you give freely without making me feel ashamed. I pray today for clear thinking and good judgment in my daily choices.

Help my grandkids to be smart. Give them common sense so they will not get into situations that are dangerous or wrong. When they are confused about what to do, help them think straight so they make a wise decision. Your wisdom may one day save their lives. Remind them to seek it out through your Word, prayer, and good counsel.

How can you use God's wisdom to make better choices?

Worry

Turn your worries over to the LORD.
He will keep you going.
He will never let godly people be shaken.

PSALM 55:22 NIRV

"Who of you by worrying
can add a single hour to your life?"

LUKE 12:25 NIV

Worry weighs a person down;
an encouraging word cheers a person up.

PROVERBS 12:25 NLT

Do not worry about anything, but pray and ask God for everything you need, always giving thanks. And God's peace, which is so great we cannot understand it, will keep your hearts and minds in Christ Jesus.

PHILIPPIANS 4:6-7 NCV

God, you've given us the solution for the problem of worry. Rather than ask you to remove our worries, you've told us to turn them over to you in prayer and thanksgiving. Your peace will then settle in and stand watch at the doorway of our souls. Today I turn my worries about my future, my financial situation, and my health over to you. I will not allow them to wear me down. Instead I will let your peace keep constant guard over my heart and mind as I rest in you.

Deliver my grandkids from anxiety. New situations can be scary: meeting new people, worrying about mom and dad when they're not home, the fear of being left or getting lost, the fear of failure. I pray today that you would help them see that worrying doesn't change anything. Remind them to talk to you about everything and receive your peace.

What worries can you hand over to God today?

BroadStreet Publishing Group, LLC.
Savage, Minnesota, USA
Broadstreetpublishing.com

Prayers & Promises for Grandmas

978-1-4245-5846-9 (faux)
978-1-4245-5847-6 (ebook)

Prayers composed by Diane Dahlen.

Design by Chris Garborg | garborgdesign.com
Compiled and edited by Michelle Winger | literallyprecise.com

Printed in China.
19 20 21 22 23 5 4 3 2 1

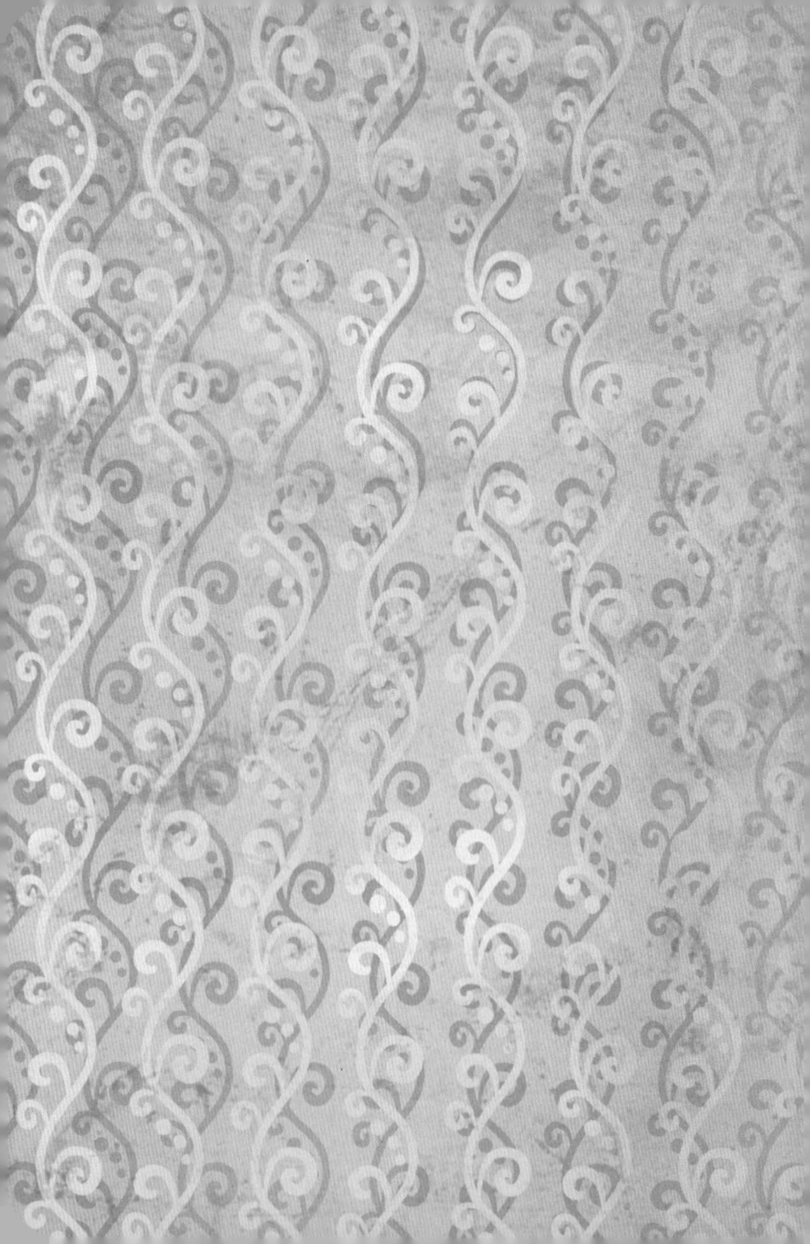